The Branding Handbook

THE ULTIMATE BRAND BUILDING GUIDE

By

Cloe Luv

TABLE OF CONTENTS:

Introduction

Introduction:

When you hear the words Coca Cola or iPhone, what is the first image that comes to your mind? A red and white cursive logo or an apple emblem, respectively. That is the power of strong branding, my friend. The term "brand" is broad. It encompasses many different things, from a name and logo to its services, quality of products, mission statement and company culture. With just a simple logo or marketing campaign, you cannot develop a brand. Developing a brand includes a myriad of steps and intricate procedures. Having a brand name, an identity, does not happen overnight. Knowing the right color scheme for the logo, or having a deft graphic designer might help you with the visuals, but does it encourage returning customers and dignified word of mouth? That requires strategic planning and critical analysis of your brand setup. It requires a team of dedicated professionals with good communication, who have a sound knowledge of your brand, and those, who are not afraid to toy with the unknown. With millions of brands trying to make a name for themselves in the market, it can be hard to differentiate yourself from others, celebrate your individuality and build a unique identity. If you are stuck in such a rut or are a budding entrepreneur looking to build your brand from scratch, you have come to the right place. In this book, I won't only be defining the parameters of building a brand but discussing what a successful brand is and looks like to a consumer. Without further ado, let's get into it!

Chapter 1: Understanding the Basics of a Brand

Whether you plan on creating a brand identity for yourself or for a client, it is important to know what a brand is to truly comprehend its prerequisites.

What is a Brand?

A brand is the heartbeat, image and 360-degree level of integrity associated with any product/service manufactured/provided by a particular business. A brand is not the sign, label, logo, name, or slogan which differentiates its products from its competitors, but much more than that. To create a brand identity, a combination of all these elements is required. The word brand came from a historical practice where cattle breeders would 'brand' their cattle to define ownership. You could therefore equate it with a trademark. A trademark is the legal security granted to a brand name.

A brand is seen as one of the most important assets of a company. It reflects the company's face, an identifiable emblem, slogan, or symbol. The public identifies your wares by this brand name. The brand oftentimes also refers to the business, and thus, they become one and the same. This brand name comes with a stock market monetary value (if the company is public), which influences stockholder shares as they rise and fall. It is important to maintain the credibility of the brand for these reasons.

Building a Brand:

When a company wishes to settle on the public image of a brand, it must first establish its brand identity or how it wants to be perceived. A company logo, for instance, also incorporates the message, slogan, or product that the company provides. The aim is to make the brand unforgettable and enticing to the customer. To come up with ideas for the visual elements of a brand, such as the logo or emblem, the company usually consults a design firm or a design team. A good brand accurately reflects the message or feeling that the business is seeking to get across and results in brand awareness, or the acknowledgement of the presence of the brand and what it provides. An unsuccessful brand, on the other hand, sometimes results from miscommunication.

The business is said to have established brand value once a brand has generated positive sentiment with its target audience. Microsoft,

Coca-Cola, Ferrari, Apple, and Facebook are some examples of businesses with strong brand value.

If done correctly, for not only the product being marketed, but also for other goods sold by the same company, a brand identity results in an increase in sales. A good brand increases trust and the consumer is more likely to try another product by the same brand after having a good experience with one product. This is sometimes referred to as brand loyalty. To sum up, building a brand requires a cohesive team to come together and work for generation of greater revenue and returning customers. This process has three main steps:

Having a sound, grip on your brand strategy, identity and marketing can help you make an everlasting impression on your customers and build a legacy. But there are so many more benefits of brand building.

Importance of Brand Building:

Some businesses' reluctance to invest in branding often comes down to a matter of perception. Drawing clear connections between good branding and quantifiable returns is not easy. But the simple truth is that you cannot put a price on the importance of creating a genuinely great brand.

So, what is the importance of investing in branding? "Investment" is the operative word here. Branding is seen by so many firms as just another cost counted against their marketing budget. But you see that it is more than just an added expense when you realize how integral branding is to shaping customer behavior. It is a long-term strategy that over the life of your business will produce measurable returns. Looking at just five of the top returns you can get from your investment in branding.

Customer Satisfaction:

Building your brand allows you to not only draw in new customers but also ensure loyal, returning customers and provides you with the ability to tap into new markets. Loyal customers who swear by your brand will act as free marketing. They will become advocates of the brand and invite others to check you out. They will leave helpful reviews which will not only aid you in curating better products but also mitigate flaws. With brand building, you will be required to dive into your customer's demographics to make sure your product is something they resonate with. Customer research is a vital part of every branding project. In-depth interviews, focus groups, and online surveys help you to precisely define the types of customers that agree with the mission statement and values of your business. You can create clearly specified audience personas and craft marketing messaging that is explicitly targeted at your ideal customers. Ideal clients/customers are not only more likely to buy what you sell; in their partnership with your brand, they are also far more loyal.

Less Investment in Marketing:

If a brand is already held in high regard by the public, you will not be required to spend additional in money on marketing. Your existing marketing campaigns would become a breeze if your brand were coherent and well-articulated, and you can only achieve that if you follow the strategies of brand building. Branding requires you to identify your key messaging, identity of the brand, and role in the marketplace. The consumer research involved in branding, as I have just described, helps you to establish targeted marketing strategies that are highly relevant to your most significant customer segments. A bold new identity makes every marketing touchpoint more engaging, while the branding guidelines and models will save you time and money on all your future initiatives' content.

Close More Deals:

Ask any salesperson on the frontlines of commission warfare and they will tell you: it's just easier to sell well-defined, strategically placed products. If your entire workforce is well-versed on what your mission statement is, what your brand represents, what your customers want, and what is their demographic and their likings are, it will be easier to curate a new product and consequently sell it to them. This all comes with efficient and adequate brand building. This takes a big weight off the shoulders of the sales team because before they connect with potential clients, a large portion of their work has already been done. Branding offers a unique benefit to your sales team, helping them to close more deals easily and comfortably.

Command Higher Prices:

What they say is true: clients do not buy goods, they buy labels. Consumers are prepared to pay higher rates for products that they consider superior. It will cost you around $5 for a white t-shirt from Hanes. A white t-shirt with an Armani tag will run you north of $150. Efficient branding helps you to place your business as a market leader with value propositions that cannot be delivered by any of your competitors. Tangible value is built into this form of meaningful distinction. This solidifies your worth and enables you to command better prices for your products or services.

Boost Company Value

Never underestimate the strength of the equity of brands. It can also have a positive impact on your share price, in addition to justifying higher price points on your offerings. Higher financial output is realized through stronger brands. The long-term outcome of strong branding is that when you are ready to exit, your business itself is worth more. Not unlike the cost of home construction, when the time comes to negotiate a purchase price, an investment in branding delivers valuable returns.

As Jeff Bezos says, "Branding is what people say about you when you are not in the room."

Types of Brands:

When it comes to developing a brand, you must know your brand type. This will only help you in deciding your brand strategy, which is the first step of the process. A brand is more than just the logo, slogan, or even the name of your company. A branding approach includes identifying the intent, target market, and value proposition of the business.

You need to build brand value once you have established what you stand for. This clearly demonstrates to clients that certain brand values are not merely hollow terms. Building a brand and generating brand equity requires time and money. All the name recalls and repetitive business that will result is worth the investment.

To create brand awareness, different businesses will need different approaches to branding. I examine methods of branding in this guide, so you understand what they are and how they can be leveraged to help you achieve your business goals.

Types of brands include:

Individual Brands:
A tangible, individual product, such as a car or

drink, is the most common type of brand. This can be very basic, such as the tissue brand Kleenex, or it can include a wide variety of items. A number of offerings, such as Mercedes S-class cars or all types of Colgate toothpaste, can also be associated with product brands.

Some businesses have a different name for each of their products and services. This may create a public perception of competition among a company's different sub brands, such as with various soft drinks created by the same company. Individual branding may also be used to distinguish various parts of a company, particularly if they span several different areas, such as in the food and clothing sectors.

Sometimes perceived brand rivalry when two different products from the same company are branded differently, helps that company gain extra market share. This is commonly done by large corporations, and if the new brand takes business away from the one on which the business is founded, it is a risky move.

Service Brands:
When businesses shift from manufacturing products to delivering full solutions and intangible services, a service brand evolves. The need to

maintain a consistently high standard of service delivery characterizes service brands. The following are included in this category:

- Brands with classic operation (such as airlines, hotels, car rentals, and banks)

- Pure service suppliers (such as member associations)

- Brands of professional services (such as all types of consultants: accountancy, management consultancy)

- Agents (such as travel agents and estate agents)

- Brands in retail (such as supermarkets, fashion stores, and restaurants)

Organizations Brands:
Organizations Brands are firms and other organizations that provide goods and services. Mercedes and the United States Senate each have strong organizational brands, and each has associated characteristics that make up its brand. It is also possible to associate organizations closely with an individual's brand. In U.S. government, for instance, The Democratic Party is closely aligned with Barack Obama and Bill and Hillary Clinton.

Personal Brands:

It is possible to consider an individual a brand. As in the case of Oprah Winfrey or Mick Jagger, it can be made up of one person. Or it can be comprised of a few people, where various identities are associated with the branding. The phenomenon of personal branding provides instruments and strategies for almost everyone to build a brand around themselves with the advent of the Internet and social media.

Group Brands:

When a small number of branded organizations have overlapping, intertwined brand equity, group branding occurs. The OWN community brand of the Oprah Winfrey Network, for instance, is closely associated with the brand of its well-known members (Oprah and her team). Similarly, the Rolling Stones are a community brand closely aligned with its members' personal brands (most enduringly, Mick Jagger, Keith Richards, Ronnie Wood, and Charlie Watts).

Events Brands:

When they aim to provide a consistent experience that attracts customer loyalty, events may become brands. Examples include TED series conferences; music festivals such as Coachella or the media convention brand SXSW; sporting events such as the Olympics or NASCAR; and traveling musicals like Wicked on Broadway. These brands' strength depends on the experience of the people attending the case. Savvy brand managers from product, service and other brand forms recognize the power of event brands and pursue sponsorships to align their brands with the event brands. Event sponsorship is now a big industry that is flourishing.

Geographic Location Brands:
Many places or regions of the world are seeking to market themselves to raise awareness for the vital qualities they offer. Branded places can vary from towns, streets, countries, states, and even individual houses (think the *Playboy* mansion). Geographic branding is also used to attract trade and economic activity, licensing opportunities, retail sales, tourism, new inhabitants, etc.

Private-Label Brands:
Among retailers with a particularly strong identity, private-label labels, also called own brands, or store brands, exist (such as Save-A-Lot). For a quality product, private labels may denote superior, "select" quality, or lower cost.

Media Brands:

Newspapers, magazines, and news networks such as CNN are among media brands.

E-Brands:

Only in the virtual world do E-brands exist. Many e-brands, such as Amazon, focus mainly on the provision of an online front end for the provision of physical goods or services. To help customers, some provide information and intangible resources. The emphasis on offering a valued service or experience in the virtual world is usually a prevalent denominator among e-brands.

Chapter 2: Building Brand Strategy

Most people automatically think of a logo, colors, and fonts - the visual aspects of a brand - when you think of "Branding." Yet the idea of branding has so much more to it.

A brand is the idea or perception that people have in mind when thinking about a company's specific products, services, and activities, both in a realistic (e.g., "the gloves are waterproof") and emotional (e.g., "the gloves make me feel invincible to the weather") way of thinking about specific products, services, and activities. It is not just the physical attributes that build a brand, but also the emotions that people develop towards the business or its brand. When introduced to the name, logo, visual identity, or even the message conveyed, this mixture of physical and emotional signals is activated.

Simply put, your brand is your promise. Branding is the ENTIRE IDENTITY of your company. This shows the public what they should expect from your goods and services, and it lets you stand out from your competitors.

As I discussed before, the first step of the process is building a brand strategy. Building a brand strategy means to have a clear-cut idea of what your brand is about. What is your mission statement? What do you stand for? What are your guidelines, not only for running your brand, but product manufacturing, hiring employees, marketing, customer service, and more? For curating the perfect brand strategy, you first need brand clarity to get to this stage and beyond where you build the visual elements of your brand and slay it in your industry. If you do not have that, your company will fail, no matter how good your products or services are.

What is Brand Clarity?

Meaningful and impactful brands offer authenticity. They are self-reflective and centered on others. They remain true to themselves and work sincerely. They believe in their importance and significance and express it to their audience, clearly. They relate emotionally to their audience and they provide a solution to the concerns of their audience. You need to take a big step back to get clear on *why* before you spend precious time and money creating a brand, marketing, acquiring a new company, expanding your online space, or developing new products and services. You need to dig deep down into who you are here to help to be effective. Attaining brand clarity is like doing the rough work for setting a mission statement and consequently a brand guideline. It helps you define your message both internally and externally. Your message must remain consistent with not only your primary targeted customers and workforce but also to your secondary and tertiary targets, competitors, and potential employees.

You've got to ask yourself

- Does my brand represent the values and ambitions of my company? And does it resonate with my ideal clients' principles and requirements?

- How can I differentiate myself from the competition? What makes my organization unique? How am I revolutionizing my sector?

- What is the process? How do I constantly change myself?

- Do I work for the customer's satisfaction only or am I truly following my passion in this brand building?

- Is my message visible to all? Is it consistent across all platforms? Do people connect with the products and services of my company?

- Am I consistent in my marketing both online and offline?

If your brand is not aligned in this manner, then how can you be sure that you are creating a future for your business, your industry, or your client?

The Power of Brand Strategy:

When you know why you get out of bed every morning to do what you do, when customers trust what you stand for more than just taking their money, you can encourage people to want your brand in their lives and empower others to help achieve your vision. A brand strategy is like a map; a blueprint without which a house cannot be built.

When a new version of an iPhone is launched, just look at the lines outside of an Apple store - even when the latest iteration is not a big leap from the last one. That is the power of a strong brand that is straightforward about its mission and values and knows its audience.

Without brand transparency, you will find that consumers will prefer others over you. They will resonate with those who have a well identified target audience, those who know where they are going, have a powerful set of values, and know how to relate to their audience in an authentic way.

And I will not lie. It can be hard, time-consuming, and unpleasant to define your brand. It is like a journey of self-discovery. It requires that you answer the following questions:

- What is the purpose of your company?
- What are the advantages of your goods or services and their features?
- What are your clients and prospects already thinking about your business?
- What attributes do you want them to associate with your business?
- What are the fundamental principles you have?
- Who is your target audience?

What Stage Are You at?

As business owners, on our path towards business success, we are all in slightly different positions. You can have complete clarity about your business vision and target audience. That is, you know *why* you do what you do, not just what you do, and you know exactly for whom you do it. But you lack a simple understanding of the identity and values of your brand: you do not know how to interact with your audience or understand how anything you do affects your overall value proposition.

Although other organizations may be clear about their principles and vision, it needs support to identify its target audience and how to interact with them, including, more importantly, getting consistency on its website: identifying the content and functionality that will resonate with the audience and the needs of the audience.

Of course, whether you are just starting out in your company or your company is founded but struggling to be consistent and coherent, you may need consistency in all areas.

Defining Parameters:
I asked you a bunch of questions in the last section. It is time for you to answer those questions to develop a brand strategy. Sit down

with likeminded people or people with stakes in the company and start answering the questions.

Having trouble attaining full clarity?

Lucky for you, I know how clarity can be accomplished! You need to critically analyze yourself and what requires revision; do a full assessment. How is your brand perceived internally and externally? It should be an accurate and honest reflection. Set up a brand audit questionnaire. Everyone should fill out this questionnaire, be it your internal team, brand employees, stakeholders or even customers. It should do a deep dive into every aspect of your brand including your values, brand personality, logo, and market positioning. There are a lot of DIY (do it yourself) choices out there on how to get brand clarification and it is a perfect idea if you're the DIY kind and have the time to spend on it. Bear in mind, to achieve the whole overview of brand transparency, you will have to piece various things together. But make sure you have all the bases covered.

Question: Who are you?
You must answer the main broad question, "Who are we?" Anything short and simple is the best response.

No matter how nuanced the truth is, the brand's keynote must be instantly graspable if it is to have true influence.

We are often asked to do a project without first getting a chance to do brand creation work. "We just need a new website that expresses it better, oh, our brand's fine." This almost always leads to issues because more often than not, a spruced-up website cannot fix the lack of brand clarity.

In reality, the ability to reduce your brand messaging to one word is a sign of brand power.

- Toyota: reliable

- Mercedes: prestigious

- BMW: driving

- Volvo: safety

Each company has grown its brand into a single word that distinguishes it from its competitors. A brand is often composed of several elements: colors, words, images, logos, advertisements, all without strategic direction in the course of time. Consequently, a clear and cohesive message is not reflected or amplified.

A brand cannot be many different things if it is to be strong. You should have the courage to disregard those who are always going to whisper, "But that too is important." To catch this urge is a formula for brand mediocrity: in many such situations, everything is there, and everything is real and yet, in short, nothing sticks into the mind of the consumer. Therefore, let me ask the question again. "Who are you? And "What do you most care about?"– the one thing that best represents you and which is most important to your audience.

Make the decision, so we can place it all below. Once every brand feature aligns and everyone refers to the ONE thing...

Understanding Target Markets:

You need to have an understanding of your audience before you start anything else. Therefore, conduct thorough market research. An audience gives you better marketing opportunities. For example, if you are selling a piece of digital equipment, your target audience is probably technicians, hence you will need to use terms and visuals which resonate with them. This is why most kid's products engage the use of cartoons to attract young minds. The best way to learn about your audience is to buy questionnaires, industry trends, and communication materials. Ask your desired audience to fill in questionnaires and forms for you. What do they value most? Customer service, delivery time or product quality? What would they like to see more of? What is important to them when it comes to buying? Price or quality of goods/services? Keep on learning so you can better deliver. Another approach to take is constant communication. You can set up an effective communication and review center. Ask your customers to rate different aspects of your business. Ask your employees to do the same. Value your proposition and keep improving.

A goods or services performance analysis helps you decide who it is going to appeal to, and who is going to buy it in the final analysis. This is why corporations spend a great deal of time and money identifying and tracking their target market. This is because not every customer is the right fit for your goods or services.

In general, target audiences are defined by age, geographic location, annual income, and lifestyle. The concept of a specific target market helps a firm to reach and communicate with clients through sales and marketing efforts on specific market factors. Defining your target market will help you market products better too. Is your product meant for teenage children preparing for a standardized test or is it a necessity for expectant moms? Define the holistic characteristics of your typical customer.

Target market tests typically occur prior to the launch of a product or service. A company will use selective product roll-offs and focus groups during the testing process to offer product managers an idea of the elements of the product which are best. Upon release of a product, the company can continue monitoring its target market demographics through sales tracking, customer surveys, and other activities which enable the company to understand what its customers are demanding.

For any company, it is necessary to identify a target market, because it means the difference between selling a product or service and sitting idly by as competition increases its revenue.

It can be a huge mistake for an organization not to know its target. It can cost a company a great deal of time and resources to try to chase new clients or consumers without learning who to pursue.

It is so easy to split the goal market into different segments of the population, measured by characteristics and categories. These include gender, age, level of income, race, education, religion, marital status, and geographical location.

Consumers in these respective categories tend to value the same goods and services, so eliminating these segments is one of the key factors in deciding target markets.

Targeting a demographic not only helps with product sales as your typical customers purchase the product designed for them but ultimately, a targeted audience decides the characteristics if your products too. A target audience will help you tweak your business strategy, brad identity, and marketing to fit their needs. This will ensure that people connect more with your product and leave a more lasting impression.

In a marketing plan which identifies other key factors for the product, such as distribution, pricing, and promotion efforts, the target market is central. The target market also defines essential product factors. Indeed, certain elements of a product, including the amount of sugar in the soft drink, can be modified by a company so that customers of different preferences are more likely to buy it.

As the product sales of a business increase, it may also extend its international target market. International expansion enables a business in various parts of the world to enter a wider subset of its target market.

A business will also see its domestic target market grow as its goods become more attracted on the market, in addition to international expansion. Enhanced and rising target markets give businesses more incentive to track revenue and consumer desires in the light of changing income opportunities.

Differentiate Yourself From the Competition:

When you are conducting a market research it is important to learn about your competition too. This is important for various reasons. Not only will this help you identify which features you both share, but also identify which features are different form each other. You can then use it as a marketing ploy and incorporate the differences in, not only your advertising, but also your strategy. Moreover, it will give you grounds on which you can improve, excel at, and get ahead of your competition. You can offer more by keeping an eye on them.

If you are just starting out, this is even more of an asset to you. By studying their market practices, you can learn what works and what doesn't without having to experience it for use of and lose capital in the process. It can help you in competitively setting the price of your edict and choosing brand ambassadors of the product.

To elaborate, when it comes to marketing, there are many different approaches that you can take. This will be talked about later. However, once such approach is hiring influencers, artists, and other famous people to endorse your brand. This requires you to carefully select people who will not only effectively deliver your message but also resonates with the brand too. If you are selling makeup products, you would not have a chef endorse them. You would go for a makeup enthusiast. So, if you just study your competition, you will not have to spend time and energy to find people to endorse your Rodin. The work would be done for you.

A SWOT Analysis:
A SWOT analysis is another great way to define the characteristics of your company. It means

knowing your strengths. What are your pros? What advantage do you have over your rivals? What sets you apart? What positive feedback do you get from your customers?

It means defining your weaknesses. What are your drawbacks? What would you like to improve on? Where do you lack?

It also means looking for opportunities. What are changes that you can bring into you existing setup? Is your business flexible enough? Can it grow and keep up with the trends? And lastly, this analysis requires you to know the threats posed towards your business. What problems can your business typically face? A volatile market? A transportation issue, a language barrier?

Telling Your Story:
A Brand strategy is not just about developing your guidelines of to further dictate your products, marketing, and identity, but it is also valuable when telling your story. Telling your story is important because it helps people to understand if you have the same values. Are you green and sustainable or do you use high end products to create the goods? Whatever the customer preference is, they can identify it by reading your

story. Your story also plays a vital part in emotionally enticing loyal customers and thus, creating a brand with a legacy.

People crave authentic interactions with brands in an age where people are tired of being spoken to and sold to. But how does the relation cultivate you? By telling the story of your brand. You can humanize your brand effectively through the story, and communicate who you are, what you do, and how you can benefit people. The more you do this, the better you can stand out and compete in the marketplace (among other benefits).

But when it comes to storytelling, just because you produce content does not mean that you tell your story effectively. Unfortunately, forsaking compelling storytelling for product-centric content that does not really connect, several brands are caught in the quantity over quality mindset.

Only 52 percent of marketers regularly use storytelling in their marketing, according to the Content Marketing Institute's 2019 B2C Content Marketing Trends.

This is a major missed opportunity. It is important to tell your brand story for ads, but it can also help you otherwise.

The Science Behind a Brands Story:

Why is storytelling so strong? Since a biological reaction is activated. A brand story draws interest, elicits an emotion, and engages individuals, and it goes across all media for storytelling. Your brain physically reacts to it when you are engaged in a good story.

A good story will cause the brain to release cortisol or oxytocin in (the stress chemical) (the feel-good chemical). This explains why you feel nervous when watching a horror movie or satisfied when at the end of a book the lovers finally get together.

And different mediums and tools for storytelling influence us in various ways. Video, for instance, induces emotional contagion, a process in which our emotions mimic what we see on television (again, think of the horror film response). Similarly, it induces neuronal coupling when we hear someone talking, such as a narrator in an animated film, an event where our brain activity mirrors what a speaker is saying.

It is not just about seeing pictures or hearing a human voice, though; it is the main story that matters. If you can tell a convincing story about a company, individuals are automatically captivated. Whether it is the story of how you created your company or the story of how your product enhances the lives of people, one of the most successful ways to attract, interact, and inspire people to develop a relationship with your brand is to find a unique brand story.

Essentials of a Great Brand Story:
To do this well, of course, you need to understand what makes an impactful brand story (specifically your brand story). It essentially comes down to five elements. You will set your brand up for success from the jump when you tell tales that fall into these categories.

It Makes Sense. All struggles with the shock of content. There are a million labels, jumping on whatever bandwagon their rivals are on, competing for publicity. Therefore, so many brands concentrate on what they want to create (or what other brands create) and not what individuals really care about. It has to be interesting and important to the individuals you are trying to attract if you want to tell a good story.

They Are Personal. You can tell tales of all kinds. They can be fun, educational, or motivational. Yet individuals need to feel connected to them personally. This is crucial not only to pique interest, but also to draw them into the story. How do they better their lives with your brand? Why are they expected to take the time to invest in this tale? Remember: If someone in your story has no location, there is no need for them to pay attention to it.

They Are Sentimental. Emotion and empathy are all about stimulating a good brand narrative. It is not only about what you are doing, but how people are influenced by you. Sure, emails can be automated by the machine, but it makes life simpler and stress-free for people. That is the story's emotional hook. You will have them hooked if you can activate the emotion in the first paragraph of a blog or the first few seconds of a video.

It is Straightforward. Trying to say too much is one of the most prevalent errors in brand storytelling. It is much easier than bombarding individuals with multiple stories to tell a clear story and optimize emotional connection. You might tell a tale about the healthcare industry's large-scale issues but showing how these problems impact a particular patient gives the story a special emphasis and makes it easier to communicate with. In short, concentrate on one person or one issue at a time, so that the reader is not confused or distracted.

It is Real. When you share a story about your brand, people should know that it is your story. That means being clear, truthful, and available. It implies letting shine through your personality. It implies being reliable, too. It is important to cultivate consistency when you produce a lot of content so that people can not only recognize your content but trust it.

How To Tell a Brand Story?

A brand story does not only grace the about section of your website but is something you can use in marketing as well.

If you are looking for ways to tell the story of your brand through content, I can quickly and easily get you started. I have outlined the measures to be taken here to ensure that you tell stories that accurately represent your brand and comply with your long-term objectives.

Step 1: Know Your Own Story
One of the greatest challenges to telling the brand story is not knowing who you are, what you do, what you care about, and why it matters about your own brand. Without this clarification, telling the right stories in the right way is hard. So, it is important to go back to basics before you start brainstorming ideas.

Define the Heart of the Brand. To define your core principles (purpose, vision, mission, and values. **Articulate your messaging for your brand**. If you want to tell the story of your company, clear messaging is key. **Know your goal.**

Step 2: Brainstorm Brand Story Ideas:
You have a fascinating brand story, no matter your product, service, or industry. (You have a few, actually.) You just need to take a step back sometimes and look at your day-to-day business. I think that many amazing stories are always waiting to be revealed, but brands do not always know how to discover them.

I find it helpful to brainstorm about particular aspects of your brand when you are trying to come up with ideas. To help jumpstart these thoughts, I would like to ask you the same few questions.

1) Who Are You?

You're not a company that is faceless. Your brand was started by a real individual (or people). In your workplace, real people are working, producing your product, and running your social media. One of the best ways to cultivate a bond is to put a face to your brand, so consider ways you could peel back the curtain to show people who you are, what your culture is like, and what you care about.

This type of content is particularly fun to produce because it provides an opportunity to really inject the personality of your company, thinking of things like spotlights behind the scenes, employee showcases, favorite things, etc.

2) What Are You Doing?

Think about the item or service that you have. Beyond conventional promotional materials, there are many ways to communicate about or display these highlights.

Are there specific features that make it especially useful or productive for your product? Are there unexpected ways in which individuals benefit from your service? You can create fun content with a little imagination, which highlights your brand in exciting ways.

Note: It is a good way to do this to tell a brand story that begins with a problem or question, so conflict generates a bit of stress or suspense. Your story will also have feel-good oxytocin if you can show your product as the "hero" and have a satisfactory resolution. (You could hear the tale, for example, of how your security software protected the small business of a family from identity theft.)

3) For Whom Are You Doing It?
Think of the individuals you want to support. These are the individuals whose company you are seeking to win. Why do they care for you? How would you want them to help? Think of not just what you are doing, but how it enhances the lives of people. For starters, if your app makes it easy for people to book holidays, it is essentially so that you can really help people relax and enjoy life.

4) Why Are You Doing That?
If you are a small start-up or an established brand created a century ago, no matter your product or service, there is a reason you exist, and, most

definitely, a higher purpose. You secure property and give people peace of mind if you are a home protection company. You have nutritious treats to nourish the bodies of your customers if you are a granola bar company.

To sum up, a brand strategy is all about the aim of a brand, its values, its commitment to its cause and communication, and promise to customers. Your vision, goals and purpose will help dictate your brand guidelines which are necessary to not only keep your internal team on one page but let the customers know what they are getting themselves into. If you still do not have a clear idea, then you can study Skype community guidelines. This is a basic framework which any organization can follow. You can form a creative brief from here to ensure everyone is on the same page aligned towards the same goal. Next you need to visually brainstorm. Write down the first thing that comes to your mind when you say your company's name. Is it fast delivery? What is fast? A cheetah, perhaps? You are already building brand identity. And this is why brand strategy and messaging are the first steps. Knowing your personas will help you stick to your goal but also determine what your customers engage with. A strategy will ensure that your identity is a product of your brand values and is something your customers would want to invest in. It will produce a framework for unique product developed, form the basis of customer interaction, govern marketing policies.

Lastly, before starting, remember to have a team which works together cohesively. Hire people whose values resonate with your brand. Keep defining your team into segments dedicated to different tasks. Make sure each team is fully efficient and working in a manner which increases overall productivity and lets each team shine. Engage in trust and team building exercises. Keep moving people around. Make sure you communicate properly and express appreciation with positive feedback, to keep morale high. Employees should be reporting on each other too to make sure a healthy environment is maintained, and no one is discriminated against. I would suggest you study the Six Sigma policy if you are having internal issues.

Chapter 3: What is Brand Identity?

A brand identity is anything which depicts the personality of your brand. It is everything from the right colors, imagery, visuals, typography to the right voice, commitment, and communication.

History of Brand Identity

Millennia ago, national, religious, guild, and heraldic symbols were branding. This has become modern branding. Modern practice dates to the industrial revolution; however, producers found a way to distinguish themselves from rivals as household products started to be manufactured in factories.

Thus, these attempts progressed from basic visual branding to commercials that included mascots, jingles, and other methods of sales and marketing. Bass Brewery, the British brewing firm, and Tate & Lyle, the food-processing company, both claims to have the oldest brands. Other brands that emerged include Quaker Oats, Aunt Jemima, and Coca-Cola in that era.

Brand identity is a brand's recognizable elements that define and differentiate the brand in the minds of customers, such as color, style, and logo. Brand identity varies from brand image. The first is consistent with the branding intention and the manner in which a business operates – all to promote an image in the minds of consumers:

- Choose its name

- Design its logo

- Use colors, shapes, and other visual elements in its products and promotions

- Craft the language in its advertisements

- Train employees to interact with customers

The brand image is a successful or ineffective outcome of these efforts.

Brand Identity Awareness

Brand identity awareness effectively generates the public impression that its products/services are smart, creative, state-of-the-art, and incredibly useful. Apple Inc. is still the leading brand identity company in a recent survey for most powerful and well-loved brands. The personality and image of Apple's brand have been closely aligned.

At the same time, a positive brand identity can be created which cannot translate into a positive brand picture. Some pitfalls are known and attempts by legacy brands to draw on a new or demographic generation are particularly misleading. The 2017 ad of PepsiCo, Inc. showed a non-specific rally that seemed to allude to the Black Lives Matter, the vibrant police brutality campaign. As a spokesperson subsequently described it, the brand identity it wanted to project was "a global message of unity, peace, and understanding."

Instead, as The New York Times put it, the commercial was widely disparaged for "trivializing" Black Lives Matter. The moment in the commercial, where a white actress gives a Pepsi to a police officer and appears to settle all the complaints of the fictional demonstrators, became the subject of intense critique immediately.

The sales of Pepsi do not seem to have been directly impacted by this gaffe, but a negative difference between brand identity and brand image can impact financial results in some instances. When its once iconic brand became synonymous with garish logos, low design, oversexed advertisements, and plain meanness, the teen apparel retailer Abercrombie & Fitch experienced a serious downturn. For example, their "We go after the attractive all-American kid with a great attitude and a lot of friends," brand identity, the chief executive officer (CEO) said, the company declined to sell women's clothing size XL or larger. "A lot of people don't belong, and they can't belong."

Building a positive brand image will, by the same token, bring steady sales and make product rollouts more effective. In the launch of two new subscription-based music streaming services in 2015, an indication of the advantages of brand loyalty is seen. Because of brand loyalty, Tidal and Apple Music had to make different decisions in the marketing and rollout of their services. Apple, an existing brand with very loyal customers, did not have to invest in Tidal's style of celebrity-oriented marketing to support its new service.

Identity of a Brand and Reputation:

A good brand can be one of the most valuable assets of the business, beyond saving the company money on marketing. Brand worth is intangible, making quantification difficult. Still, the cost of building a comparable brand, the cost of royalties to use the brand name, and the cash flow of comparative unbranded companies are taken into account in traditional approaches.

Building Brand Identity:

The steps a business should take to create a solid, coherent, and reliable brand identity will vary, but for most, a few points apply broadly:

Analyze the organization and the market. A complete SWOT review involving the whole business, a look at the strengths, limitations, opportunities, and risks of the company, is a proven way to help managers understand their situation so that they can better assess their objectives and the measures needed to accomplish them.

Determine main business priorities. The personality of the brand should help achieve these objectives. For example, if an automaker is targeting a luxury niche market, it should craft its advertising to cater to that market. On networks and places where potential customers are likely to see them, they should appear.

Identify its clients. It can help a business define its target audience by conducting surveys, convening focus groups, and having one-on-one interviews.

Determine the character and meaning that it wants to convey. Instead of attempting to combine any imaginable positive trait: utility, affordability, efficiency, nostalgia, modernity, luxury, flash, taste, and class, an organization needs to build a clear perception. A cohesive message should align and produce all elements of a brand, such as copying, imagery, cultural allusions, and color schemes.

Building a brand identity is a multi-disciplinary strategic endeavor, and the overall message and business objectives need to be supported by any aspect. It may include the name, logo, and design of a company; its style and tone; the look and composition of its products; and, of course, its appearance in the social media. In Apple shops, Apple founder Steve Jobs was famously fascinated with information as tiny as the shade of gray on bathroom signs. Although there may be no need for that degree of emphasis, the anecdote indicates that the good branding of Apple is the product of concerted effort, not serendipity.

Why is Brand Identity Important?

1. Personality: The visual representation of the values and "personality" of your brand is a brand identity. Identity design essentially sets the tone of your brand, and it can be used in your audience to evoke particular feelings. To communicate the overall message of your company and promote your business goals, your brand identity should be designed.

2. Consistency: You can build a consistent message across all marketing materials by developing a brand identity. Each piece, creating a cohesive branding package, should have the same fundamental styles and design elements.

3. Differentiation: A brand identity lets you distinguish your company from the competition and position the brand appropriately. Developing a professional, innovative identity design can help you stand out in your market to potential customers.

4. Awareness: Creating a package of brand identity ensures that all your marketing materials are at the forefront of your brand, which helps to increase brand awareness. The more places your brand is featured, the more it will make interaction with buyers, and the more it will be unforgettable.

5. Loyalty: An efficient brand identity can help build a brand's customer loyalty and trust, as it allows customers to create a link between a product and the business.

Brand Vs Brand Identity

The terms brand/branding, brand identity is falsely put in the same basket as they were synonymous. There are a lot of misconceptions. It is true that they all work together, but they are distinct at their core. You may see that some people are trying to be philosophical about all these terms, and they may seem harder to understand than they really are.

You need to have a strong, consistent, and thoughtful brand/branding and brand identity, not just a logo design, to have a solid business. For each blogger, creative entrepreneur, or small business owner, this is absolutely must-have knowledge. Many company owners neglect their branding and underestimate the strength of it. I cannot remember the many times I have heard the question, "Do I really need a brand?" Is a logo not enough? or "can't I just get myself branded later?"

I am absolutely passionate about branding and I could go on and on and realize that on my blog I haven't really shared enough about branding, so I'm so excited to talk to you about all those things! Today, you will learn what branding is, what a brand identity is, and what the difference between brand identity and logo design is. Let's just dive in, shall we?

What Does Branding/Brand Mean?

I would say branding is an experience if you were to ask me to explain branding (or brand) in one word. Branding consists of the mission, core values, visions, company voice of your company, so it is like a huge customer experience plan. It is the way you make the target audience feel, it is a psychological relationship with business and the customer, what they imagine in their minds when they think of your business.

The brand is an integral part of your company, the personality of your company (if you are a solopreneur, it could be your personality), the style (both tangible and intangible, such as the way you speak/write) and the promise of what your client will experience from your company.

The branding allows you to shape your company with more variables than just a visual aspect. This helps you distinguish your goods and services from your rivals. Your brand strategy includes how, what, where, when and to whom you want your brand messages and values to be communicated and delivered.

What is Brand Identity/Brand Design?

Brand identity/brand design by seeing their visuals refers to what we see and what we feel about the company (some call it visual identity). Colors, fonts, logos, alternative logos, sub marks, graphic elements, patterns, photographs are all included. The brand goes side by side with the identity of the brand and each is sometimes difficult to distinguish.

For example, let's take Dior. You can say that they want to make you feel like their brand is upscale and elegant without looking at their brand and they do not want you to mistake them for low-cost bazaar perfumes. That is why they have a simple website, using black and white or neutral colors with their iconic serif logo, using famous people in their advertisements such as Johnny Depp or Charlize Theron. With brand/branding and brand identity/brand design, this is a perfect coherence.

To create the user's experience, visual components such as logos, shapes, typography, colors, patterns, photography, packaging, and other design elements help.

The brand/branding and brand identity/brand design should work together, so even if you do not see their logo, you should be able to recognize the brand. For larger companies like Apple, Starbucks, McDonald's etc., it is certainly easier, but it is also possible for solopreneurs.

If your business is based online, it will take more time, but it is not impossible. For example, gaining the recognition of your brand identity in online companies can manifest itself by spotting someone's blog post on the Smart Feed of Pinterest and immediately thinking that that pin is from that blogger because you recognized their fonts, colors, logo, photos, or other graphic elements.

In Short, the Differences Between Branding and Brand Identity:

Branding (or brand) is intangible, which is what you want your clients to feel when they think about your company. In other words, the brand is an experience.

Brand identity (or brand design) is tangible, it is like a brand face, so it is your business's visual side.

Chapter 4: Building Brand Identity

Building a brand identity means that once you have set the strategy for your brand, you are on the road to selling your products to your desired customer base. This is where brand identity comes in. It is visually communicating your brand strategy which is a product of brand heart and brand messaging. These two comprise of your purpose, messages, values, voice, mission, and taglines. A brand identity helps to shape the opinions and view of people after the purchase. It is essentially the personality of your business. Your identity becomes what others think of you; hence it is of criticism importance. The face of your business must be your best version. It helps customer with association. If you see the Netflix logo anywhere, you will feel a certain way about that movie. Brand identity also helps people with recall and makes them believe that the product is legit. Moreover, it helps to establish credibility with competition and trust with customers once you work with consistency. You are able to secure an authoritative position in the market with authentic and strong brand identity. Your brand identity helps to spike your stocks prices. With a brand identity that is out there, you are facilitated when it comes to marketing and advertising. You are prepared to promote any and all products. You know the framework of your brand identity and guidelines so all that is left to do is get creative. You have a ready-made template, put it to use anytime. No need to work your way from the ground up and invest in more time, money and effort which is of essence in all businesses. A company's mission becomes evident to all through its identity. You can celebrate your values and practices. Your purpose is known to you, your workers, your buyers, your competitors and to the market. If it is something that resonates with people, they will be attracted to it. And the existing customer base will feel reaffirmed in their standing and feel a sense of belonging with your brand. This is what makes the difference in the end. A good brand makes advocates of its brand, whereas a good product only brings in customers. You need advocates to attract more customers and ensure returning customers. Once you know your business inside out, it is time to bring it alive. The main components are color scheme, logo, typography design system, photography, illustrations, data visualization, iconography, interactive elements, web design, video, and motion.

Color Psychology

One of the most interesting and most controversial aspects of marketing is the psychology of color as it relates to persuasion.

What is the Psychology of Color?

Color psychology is the study of how perceptions and behaviors are affected by colors. In marketing and branding, color psychology focuses on how colors impact the impressions of consumers and whether they persuade consumers to consider or make a purchase from specific brands.

When creating marketing assets, building a new business, or rebranding an existing one, it is an important field of study to consider. Consider this: Researchers found that up to 90 percent of snap judgments made about products can be based on color alone in a study titled "Impact of color on marketing."

The bottom line is that your brand does not have clear-cut guidelines for choosing colors. "While simply looking at an infographic and making the right decision would be nice, the reality is that the answer to "What colors are right for my brand? "Always is, "It depends."

The answer is frustrating, but it is the truth. The context within which you operate is an essential consideration. What matters is the feeling, mood, and image that your brand or product creates.

The good news: research into color psychology can assist you to make the right choice.

The right color is suitable for your brand. Researchers found in a 2006 study that the relationship between brands and color depends on the perceived appropriateness of the color being used for the specific brand. In other words: Does that color fit what is being sold? Research has found that predicting consumer reaction to color appropriateness is far more important than the individual color itself when it comes to picking the "right" color.

"So, ask yourself (or better yet, gather customer feedback) when considering colors for your marketing and branding: "Is this color suitable for what I'm selling?"

The right color reveals the personality of your brand. Due to their effect on how a brand is perceived, purchasing intent is greatly affected by colors; colors affect how customers view the "personality" of the brand in question.

And while certain colors are broadly aligned with characteristics (e.g., brown with ruggedness), almost every academic study on colors and branding will tell you that supporting the personality you want to portray is far more important for colors rather than trying to align with stereotypical color associations.

Jennifer Aaker, a psychologist, and Stanford professor has conducted studies on this very subject, and her paper entitled "Dimensions of Brand Personality" points out five core dimensions that play a role in the personality of a brand.

Brands can cross between two characteristics at times, but they are mostly dominated by one. Ask yourself: what do I want the personality of my brand to be, and how do I use color to express that personality?

The right color appeals to your audience. Joe Hallock's work on "Color Assignment" is one of the more interesting examinations of color psychology in relation to gender.

However, it is important to note that most of his respondents came from Western societies. In dictating color appropriateness for gender, one's environment, and especially cultural perception, plays a strong role, which, in turn, can influence individual color preferences.

Additional research on color perception and color preferences shows that men generally prefer bold colors when it comes to shades, tints, and hues, while women prefer softer colors. Men were also more likely to select color shades as their favorites (colors with black added), while women were more responsive to color tints (colors with white added).

While this is a hotly debated issue in the theory of color, I never understood why. Outside of gender stereotypes, brands can easily work. In fact, because they break expectations, I would argue many have been rewarded for doing so.

"Perceived suitability" should not be so rigid as to assume that a brand or product cannot succeed because the colors do not match the tastes surveyed, leading me directly into the next point...

Your brand is differentiated by the right color. Additional studies have shown that our brains prefer immediately recognizable brands, which, when creating a brand identity, makes color an important element. One journal article even suggests that picking colors that ensure differentiation from entrenched competitors is important for new brands.

You can help your brand stand out by choosing the right color. Consider the psychological principle known as the Isolation Effect: it states that it is more probable to remember an item that "stands out like a sore thumb".

Research clearly shows that when it blatantly stands out from its surroundings, participants can recognize and recall an item much better, whether it is text or an image.

Two studies on color combinations, one measuring aesthetic reaction and the other looking at consumer preferences, found that while a large majority of customers prefer color patterns with similar shades, they also favor palettes with a highly contrasting color accent.

The right color has the right name.

Although it is possible to perceive different colors in different ways, the descriptive names of those colors matter as well. According to a study entitled "A rose by any other name...," fancy names were preferred much more often when subjects were asked to evaluate products with different color names, such as makeup. For instance, even though the subjects were shown the same color, "mocha" was found to be significantly more likable than "brown."

Additional research finds that the same effect applies to a wide range of products; consumers rated paint colors that were elaborately named as more pleasing to the eye than their counterparts that were simply named.

For everything from jellybeans to sweatshirts, it has also been shown that more unusual and unique color names are preferable. "For instance, it was more likely to select crayon colors with names such as "razzmatazz" than names such as "lemon yellow.

Find a palette of your own. We are at the end of this post and there is no cheat sheet yet in sight to choose the perfect color or color scheme.

Logo:

A visual depiction of your company and brand is the logo. A graphic symbol of your brand and company is the logo. It is visual element which helps in branding. It allows for recognition of a brand due to its uniqueness and individuality. By attracting your target customers, a professional logo enables you to build a prosperous, successful business. Investing in great design will separate you from rivals, build a professional visual presence, and maintain consistency across all your company's platforms.

A logo is present almost everywhere, from your website to your business cards, products, packaging, and even on your online social media pages. Hence it must be cohesive and consistent to appear legit. We have already talked about the color. But just to reiterate the idea, colors bring out emotions. There should be one main color for your logo, 2 primary colors, 3-5 complementary colors, and 2 accents colors. Take a look at the McDonald's logo, the Golden Arches of M are not too complicated and thus have become distinguishable from any place. They key here is that once your team is briefed on the brand strategy. Give them a paper and pencil and tell them to draw the first thing that come to their mind. Keep getting feedback from customers, industry people and internal team and keep revising it till you are satisfied.

The logo is an essential part of the identity of the brand, but it is not the only element of it. Your company should represent the logo and it does not need to have dozens of other graphic elements and it does not have to be too literal.

Even without any illustrations or icons, most of the iconic logos are simple and modern. In a way that is recognizable and memorable, the logo should identify the company. Once the logo becomes familiar, by removing some of the elements, many brands simplify them.

Some brands literally have colors like you associate red with Coca-Cola and blue and red with Pepsi, so colors are more important than the logos themselves in that case, but it took time for customers to associate the colors with those brand names. You don't need to see a McDonald's logo to recognize the packaging of their products.

What Makes a Logo Stand Out?

This obviously depends on the business, audience, intended message and logo design, and the effectiveness of the logo can be quite subjective and variable across industry or company.

When creating a logo, however, there are four broad goals you should aim for:

1. It Should Be Audience-Appropriate.
Not the flashiest, but rather those that resonate with their target audience, are the best logos. Logos represent not only your business, but also the individuals to whom you are connected. The

one you speak. You would not use bright and peppy colors, for example, for a funeral home, in the same way as you wouldn't use (read: bright yellow) Depressing Grays for a party planner for kids.

2. It Should Be Simple and Clear to Read.

This is especially true for logos for wordmarks (logos that consist of text only), but it applies to every style of design. If you are forced to decipher your target audience. They will be gone faster than you can say "conversions," what your logo means. Make sure from just a glance that your logo can be easily understood. It should be easy to apply so that the designers have a clear guide on what to do.

3. This Should Be Distinct.

It is always a good starting point to draw inspiration from industry trends but remember that a logo's objective is to differentiate your brand from the competition. Distinct = unforgettable, and this is what will remind consumers that your brand is the one they should be loyal to in the industry. It should be memorable basically to leave an impact. Oh! And make sure it is cohesive. Complements all aspects of your outward expression. Craft it appropriately.

It should speak to people, fuel their emotions; this is mandatory.

4. It Should Be Scalable.

Your logo will be prominently placed across various media outlets and in various sizes, the best logos are versatile logos because of this. Those that can be easily tailored to accommodate any branding requirement you can encounter. It should be scalable and flexible. Always looking to grow and evolve.

There is a need to separate your logo from other brands, but the same does not pertain to the color scheme of your logo. Many companies gravitate between the same colors for example Netflix and YouTube. This allows new users to adjust quickly to changing landscape. However, new approach is always welcome. In 2013, Twitch came out with bold purple branding which was never done, and it turned out to be a huge success. It was bought by Amazon in the following year for 1 Billion dollars.

Website:

Your brand identity not only reflects all that your business has to offer, but also the ideals it holds dear. Just like your personal identity, what separates you from everyone else is your brand identity and your website offers you a huge opportunity to share it!

When searching for answers, one of the first places customers go is the internet, which is why it is important that your website is there to display the right message. It is necessary for your website to match your brand identity and vice versa.

The portrayal of your brand identity through a standard website template can be extremely difficult. If you cannot alter your website to the way you want it to look, how can you stand apart from others? We always recommend that you need a custom website design to ensure that you accurately reflect everything that you must give if you really want to showcase your brand. **Convey Your Calls-to-Action.** How necessary it is to motivate customers to click is overlooked by many people. Highlighting a call-to-action on each page will produce a larger number of leads, but you need to ensure that they are free from any clutter, just like your logo. Use colors, fonts and shapes that fit your brand, but they also stand out and attract the eye from the rest of the website. Tip: Not only does a call-to-action have to be, "BUY NOW" or "Order Here." You can try "Learn More" or "Let Us Help You" softer ones. **Rely on the Core**

Message. While I do not suggest that your website is a cluttered minefield of information, images, and call-to-action, I suggest that you take the focus off your website's aesthetics and think more about the core message of your company. It could mean that you will have to simplify your design, make more room for white space, and forgo your favorite colors and fonts for something that fits the overall tone to ensure that this comes across in the clearest way possible. The key place where your clients can view your brand is your website, so accuracy is extremely important. Tip: Go back to the very beginning if you do not have the key post. In the first place, why did you start this business? How would you like to make your customers feel about you? **Do Not Copy Your Competitors.** Customers who point to a competitor and request a similar website approach a number of web design firms. This can be highly damaging to your overall brand as it takes away any individuality that you might have built up through your branding attempts. Copying a rival literally means that instead of creating your own, you are unwittingly endorsing their brand!

Tip: Strive to get away from your industry while searching for inspiration. Look at random websites you may never have thought of before, which might inspire you more than your rivals.

Your website must be user friendly. Make sure there is a landing page of your website. A landing page is not the first page that the customer sees when they visit your site, but it is like of a welcome page. This is a marketing strategy. Basically, it is a page where you ask your site visitors to drop their emails so that you can market products to them later. Many people see it as a put off but what you can is, offer them a small discount to tomorrow them to drop their emails. This is the purpose of a landing page. Once they are on your sites your analytics team will track and store their activity on your site. You can use this to your advantage. when you email them altered use the pictures of the product they interacted with. Another thing to do here is to make your website more interactive. You can add in a chat box or a robot which is fed with commonly asked questions. It detects the questions of customers for keywords and answers them accurately, so customer queries are answered promptly. An FAQ section can also help users with common issues. Moreover, you can install analytics for your website. This will store the demographics of customers interacting with your brand. This information is again vital as it can potentially help you tap into new customer bases which may have been previously unknown. For example, you thought people in France were more inclined to buy your croissant mold, but maybe people in Japanese constantly using your site. Let this guide your business practice. Introduce a delivery service which ships internationally to Japan. To make your website more user friendly, add is a search bar and a drop down or side view content list and a filter menu which lets the site visitors filter between selling cost, upload date, rating and more.

As a company, the value of your website branding and how it can turn users to customers and then, in time, loyal followers of your brand should never be underestimated. Your website should clearly communicate your core values by keeping your brand name in mind and encourage your customers to interact with you on an emotional level, motivating them to make the all-important click.

Typography:

Typography is the font that you use to write your brand name in. This font type must be consistent in all your documents. Be it in your documents, business cards, print outs, files, emails, and more. Choose a font and stick to it. Take inspiration from Adidas. They keep their logo and typography the same at all places but keep toying around with the color palette.

Templates:

A template is a set design for all your printing and emailing activities. It will be used in typed letters and business cards. It includes a header, a page font and a layout. This adds to your credibility and gives the brand a more professional look. Most brands have their own set templates which are unique to them. These templates becoming the recognition of the brands at some point. Again, this should be consistent in all areas to allow harmony in identity.

Lastly, there is a proper design system that your websites, and social media pages' layouts should follow. The order of contents should be easily comprehensible in all formats, startling with headers, sub headers, body, images, blurbs and more. Photography and illustrations are main element. Visual creative media helps people connect more. On websites, people are not able to experience the product in real time so the user experience should be so immaculate that they don't feel the need. Three hundred and sixty degree images zoom in features, carousel images from different angles and accurate work duct description should be enough to do the job. Data visualization which is representation through charts and diagrams is another great branding tool. Additional elements include video, web design, interactive elements, and motion graphics.

Chapter 5: Brand Marketing

Marketing and advertising count heaps. If your marketing is impeccable, half your job is already done. Have a good graphic designing team well versed in your brand strategy to design adds be it traditions or digital and a good marketing team to not only advertise priests but also write their descriptions and target and grab the attention of the right audience. Let's be fair; not everyone in the world is the right fit for your product. Someone will buy your product, some will not. So, it's best to spend your energies in finding people who will.

Digital Media:

When you initially want to get the word for your brand out, digital media is the quickest source. While social media will help your brand reach the farthest corners of the world, no one is going to give it much heed unless you have strong support back home. Get the word out in your local community. Local news channels, talk shows, TV shows are all great ways to ensure that people in your community are hearing about your brand. Whether it is an advertisement, or product review, or customer reviews, make sure your branding is consistent and you are getting the message across. This way of marketing is especially significant of your targeted audience is more likely to spend time watching the television than pick up a phone. Lost social media users are of ages 14 to 25. Does your target audience fall in this sphere? No? Digital media is your way to go! Besides, social media requires you to create short and snappy content. It requires you to post regularly and review statistics which can be a ton of work for brands just starting out. Digital media on the other hand ensures that not only are you getting traffic, but you can have longer ads to touch all the bases. Reach out to possible news channels and TV shows that would be willing to run your ad or have on the TV to explain your brand. And voila, customers will start teaming up in no time!

Print Media:

Print Media is another great way to get the word out. No matter how much technology advances, people are still going to pick up a newspaper or magazine on their daily route of commute and read about what is happening in the world. This gives you a great opportunity to get the word out there about your business. Get a separate pamphlet added or an article written or just ad published about your brand in the newspaper or a magazine that suits your niche. You would be surprised to know that on average, statistics show that people trust printed ads more than disgusting ads. That is because of the popular saying, ''it everything on the internet is true'. People consider prints more reliable. It delivers the message and increases brand engagement. You can personalize your ad whatever way you want. Another huge advantage of print media is that print lasts longer. Your ad is going to stay in some paper somewhere till the end of time. Whereas social media ads, and digital media ads have an expiry time. They will run for some time, and then they are gone. But the sports illustration of 2013 is always going to be present in the archives or in someone's house for limitless marketing.

For both print and digital media, you will either need to reach out to TV Shows, news channels, newspaper agencies, magazines owners on your own or you can hire a publicist if you do not know where to start.

It can elevate the reputation of your business and help with increasing influence and brand reach. You can get your message across to a large audience. Publicists have connections here and there and thus can help you get on board with a few channels right away.

Hiring a publicist to do the work can be very alluring but it comes with its own set of struggles. If you are in the initial stage of your business, you might not have enough to pay for a publicist. Plus, there are no guarantees with the work they do. A news channel might pick you up if they are swayed by your brand but there is no controlling how they will portray your brand. You and the publicist cannot control that. You might not get the coverage you hoped for and you won't be able to blame the publicist for it.

Anyway, if you find a publicist that suits your pocket and has some great references, it doesn't hurt to give it a try. But know that many media outlets prefer to work directly with the person in charge. Choose wisely.

Social Media:
Social media is increasingly becoming one of digital marketing's most critical components, offering unparalleled benefits that help reach millions of clients/customers worldwide. If you don't use this lucrative source, you miss an amazing opportunity for advertisement, as it

makes it easy to spread the word about your product and your purpose.

Social media is a potent weapon in the day and age that we live in. It is digital real estate. It helps to spread the word about your new products or sales and discounts or any other news!

Gone are the days when billboards, magazines, newspapers, word of the pith, pamphlets and banners were used to advertise. Social media has quickly become the number one source of marketing because of its cheap pricing, great retargeting features, analytics services, and data storing. The brand ASOS saw a 300% rise in its profits as soon as it started making use of social media marketing. We will talk in detail about how different social media platforms can fit you and your brand, but one thing which remains consistent across all platforms is quality content. You need to churn out quality content that is relevant and relatable. Videos are more engaged by users than still posts. So, make unboxing videos, packaging videos, customer experience videos, product videos. Keep them short and snappy. Invest in good photography and videography. Make sure the lighting is right. Make sure the filters are consistent. Keep trying new things. Use trial and error to see which content is most interacted with. Consistency must be maintained that is store front and office, in printing, signage, packaging, website and online advertising, sales and customer service, internally with employees, content publishing, etc.

Improved Recognition of Brands:
One of the most stress-free and profitable tools for digital marketing that can be used to increase the exposure of your company is social media. To get started, create profiles for your company on social media and start networking with others. It will help you dramatically improve your brand awareness by applying a social media strategy. Over 91 percent of marketers said that their social media campaigns dramatically improved their brand awareness and increased user engagement by investing just a few hours per week. Undoubtedly, it would help your company to have a social media page for your brand and with a daily use, it can also create a large audience for your company in no time.

Cost-Efficient:
Social media marketing is potentially the most cost-effective tool for an advertisement campaign. For almost all social networking sites, making an

account and signing up is free. But if you plan to use paid social media ads, to see what you can expect, always start small. It is important to be cost-effective because it lets you produce a higher return on investment and keep a larger budget for other marketing and business payments. You will dramatically increase the conversion rates only by spending a little money and time and eventually get a return on investment on the money you mainly spent.

Customers Engagement:
Social networking is a fantastic way to get clients/customers involved and connect with them. The more you engage with the crowd, the more chances you have of converting. Set up a two-way contact with your target audience so that their needs are heard, and their curiosity is easily answered. In addition, contact and interaction with clients/customers

is one of the ways to draw their attention and communicate the brand message to them. Thus, in real terms, your brand can meet more markets and get founded without any hassle.

Improved Brand Loyalty:
You make it easier for your customers to find you and communicate with you when you have a

social media presence. You are more likely to improve customer satisfaction and brand loyalty by communicating with your clients/customers via social media. One of the key objectives of almost every company is to build a loyal customer base. Usually, customer satisfaction and brand loyalty go hand in hand. It is important to connect with your customers regularly and begin to build a relationship with them. Social networking is not only limited to the launch of your product, but also a leading advertising campaign medium. A consumer sees these networks as service channels where they can connect with the organization directly.

Improved Customers Satisfaction:
In networking and communication networks, social media plays a central role. In improving the overall brand image, building a voice for your business is crucial with the support of these platforms. Customers enjoy the fact that they receive a changed reply rather than a computerized response when they post comments on your website. It takes time for a brand that values its clients/customers to write a personal message that is naturally viewed in a positive light.

Consciousness of the Marketplace:

Marketplace knowledge is one of the easiest ways to discover the needs and desires of your customers instead of engaging directly with them. It is also considered social media's most important value. You will see the interest and views of consumers who you would not know otherwise if you did not have a social media presence by following the events on your profile. Social networking will help you obtain information and a greater understanding of your industry as a complementary research tool. You can then use additional resources to analyze other demographics of your customers once you get a broad following.

More Brand Authority:

Brand loyalty and customer satisfaction both play a major role in making your organization more powerful, but it all comes down to communication. It helps them to create a positive image in their minds when customers see your company posting on social media, especially responding to their queries, and posting original content. Interacting with your customers frequently shows that you and your company care for them. Once you have a few happy customers who are outspoken about their good shopping experience, you can let real customers who have enjoyed your product or service do the advertising for you.

Increased Traffic:
One of Social Media's other advantages is that it also helps boost the traffic to your website. You offer users a justification for clicking through to your website by sharing your content on social media. The more quality content you post on your social account; the more inbound traffic you can create while making opportunities for conversion.

Improved SEO Rankings:
In calculating rankings, the role of social media is becoming a critical factor. These days, SEO criteria are constantly varying to secure a good ranking. Therefore, merely improving your website and updating your blog frequently is no longer appropriate. Businesses posting their content on social media send out a search engine brand signal that speaks to the authenticity, honesty, and constancy of the business.

Marketing Your Brand:
It is a daunting challenge to build a brand from scratch. This is no mystery for those of us who have started a business or worked in a start-up

environment. To steal market, share and successfully expand, startups also challenge much greater, well-established competition, meaning long hours, innovation, and a large budget are required.

No matter the circumstances, long hours and ingenuity can be done, but not every new brand is able to rely on a large marketing budget. How do you work to develop your brand efficiently when resources are limited, which is not uncommon for new brands?

Facebook:
You need to understand the unique benefits of Facebook, and how it varies from other media, to effectively advertise your company on Facebook. You could not advertise on Facebook the way you would market in a magazine or on your website, just like you would not run a radio commercial on television.

Do not use Facebook to 'sell hard'. Facebook is seen by people as a friendly social place where they talk, check out photos and videos, and relax with friends. Instead of being a company 'outsider' who attempts to sell aggressively, you need to enter discussions and become part of a group.

Hard-selling techniques, such as using promotional slogans, constantly posting about a single product or service, or presenting lists of goods and prices in isolation from any relevant discussion, can result in you being 'unfollowed' by other users. They can even post adverse comments about your business.

Have a specific purpose and plan. It is necessary to have a clear objective and a plan for achieving that goal to use Facebook. A coffee shop, for example, could decide that its target is to increase Facebook's revenue by 10 percent in the next 6 months. Their solution may include:

- Create a post every morning with a special of the day, using a coupon code to monitor the sale to Facebook

- Posting a regular picture of a customer of the day who is its 'Coffee King or Queen'

- Encouraging customers to share their own pictures of a coffee enjoyed by them.

- Setting a target and plan provides you with guidance for your marketing on Facebook and a way to evaluate your success.

Create a human voice for your organization. Facebook users like to speak to other individuals, not to an impersonal corporation. Whoever manages your Facebook page, using a style that suits your business, must be able to write in a voice that sounds genuine and friendly. They will need permission in their own language, not in the jargon or 'official line' of the organization, to convey things.

Post Regularly. Social media is constructed around regular updates, unlike conventional media (such as magazines or television), or other online media (such as web pages).

Users of Facebook review their page more than 25 times a week, and they need to see that fresh content is updated daily. Some guides suggest posting at least once a day, but when you have interesting content, the core principles are to post and to judge how much your audience needs to hear from you.

Encourage comments and quickly respond. Encourage other users of Facebook to respond to your posts or post their own comments on your company or a subject that is of interest to them and you. When they post, respond quickly-it is best within 24 hours. Failure to react would undermine the ability of your Facebook friends to communicate with you, and they will drift away gradually.

Using videos and pictures. A big aspect of Facebook's appeal is pictures and images. To keep your mates engaged and amused, use them regularly. For instance:

- A retailer of clothing could post pictures of new stock as it arrives

- An architect or builder may post day-by-day photos of a renovated home.

- An instructional video of how to perform a specific exercise can be shared by a personal trainer.

- Get interactive with promotions, tournaments, sports, surveys, etc. When Facebook is fun, people like it, and when it offers something that they cannot get any other way.

Research shows that the most common reason for a client to follow the Facebook page of a company is for discounts and giveaways. You can also use competitions and games to liven up your website.

To distribute client surveys, Facebook can also be used. Make sure you keep surveys short if you do this, and have a survey link that users can easily press, ignore, or share with their mates.

Nurture the experiences. Building good relationships with other Facebook users takes time, so be patient. To help cultivate healthy relationships, participate genuinely in interactions, provide valuable material, and create incentives for loyal clients/customers.

Promote your Facebook page. Promote it in your company if you have a Facebook page, so that your social media works hand in hand with more conventional marketing strategies. On your letterhead, business card and website, in store, in ads, and in your email signature, include your Facebook address.

Use Facebook Insights to learn more about your customers. More about the people who want to like your page, Facebook Insights will tell you. Once you know the characteristics of your Facebook mates, you can tailor your posts and offerings to suit their needs and interests.

For example, if you are a bookstore that caters to customers of all ages, but most of your Facebook friends are between the ages of 18 and 25, your Facebook offers can focus on books suitable for that age group (while you're in-store offers are broader). Or, if you are an online seller who never sees your customer population, by reviewing their preferences, ages, and locations on Facebook, you may be able to get a better image of what they think and feel.

Instagram

With over 1 billion users, Instagram is a social media powerhouse. Simply put, it is a powerful social networking service for mobile sharing (images, videos) that allows users to take photos and short videos (maximum of one minute), then post them on other social networking sites, including Facebook, Twitter, Flickr, and Tumblr. Younger generations are potentially moving away from verbal contact, and visual media often seem enamored by the public.

For you to reach your target audience right now and transform Instagram users into traffic, subscribers, and sales for your company, there is plenty of space for growth and opportunity.

Let's look at five Instagram marketing tips that you can use on Instagram to promote your business:

1. Customize Content for Your Targeted Audience

Instagram will supplement your Facebook marketing and Twitter advertisement approaches as a predominantly visual medium. Consider how photos and beautiful graphics will draw tourists and carry them into your sales funnel, in addition to share-ability. Have a look at what the most famous brands in the world are doing to maximize their space on Instagram.

Using filters, do not forget. 'On the fly' images also appear mediocre at first glance. That is why the filtering technology of Instagram helps you to transform your photos into great-looking snapshots that attract attention - which is the first step in getting users to take action.

Also, make sure to build videos as well; Instagram has incredibly high engagement rates for videos.

2. Wisely Direct People to Your Link

Instagram does not allow picture captions (non-clickable) or comments to be hyperlinked, but you can place a link in your bio section (150 characters' maximum). This feature is used by most marketers to connect back to their company home page, or their latest marketing campaign's landing page.

You may choose to overlay a URL over an image, but it is probably easier to guide visitors to the clickable link of your bio. If you want to use paid Instagram ads, then you will have clickable links.

Note that while Instagram is a great forum for building a following and communicating with your audience, you also want to push people back to your website so that you can create your email list and generate leads and sales as well.

3. Limit the Bare Necessities Text Descriptions and Messages

Instagram does not restrict posts like Twitter does by imposing a character limit. It is in your interest, however, to let the pictures do most of the talking. Besides, the Instagram audience is not likely to defy the trend because shorter Facebook and Twitter posts attract more traffic and engagement.

Meaningful captions will provide additional insight and improve your dedication and conversion rate. If you are planning on writing longer posts, keep your captions short and punchy, or at least keep the most relevant detail at the top of the page. Most people will read what is below your pictures instantly, but fewer will enlarge the text to read something that gets cut off.

4. Maximize Opportunities for Engagement

Hashtags experiment. It is not an exact science to select the right hashtags, so look at what others are using in your niche and consult prolific bloggers who also have interesting word choices.

Accept follow requests and follow individuals with your own marketing activities that offer appealing images and teaching points. On your website and newsletters, do not forget to remind people that you are on Instagram! Add Instagram 'Follow' keys or give updates to subscribers regularly that you are providing content there. The more ways (email, Facebook, Twitter, etc.) you can reach your audience, the greater chance you would have of them hearing your message and taking the actions you want them to take.

5. Test and Track Constantly

Trends and tendencies will emerge and vanish on a dime in social media, so keep your eyes and ears open for developments and policy changes from

Instagram. Your performance quality will increase and be noticed by more tourists by trying out new choices.

Instagram provides analytical tools that aid you with performance monitoring, as with other mainstream networking sites.

LinkedIn

LinkedIn is a social network targeted towards career professionals with over 65 million users. It is a forum to promote your home company, find a job or freelance job, and connect with partners in joint ventures.

You should have a profile on LinkedIn if you have a home business that caters to other businesses (B2B) or have a business in which networking is essential for partners or customers. This guide will help if you are not there or have not maximized all the LinkedIn features. Marketing a home business on LinkedIn, like other types of internet marketing, is an affordable way to gain publicity.

Getting Started with LinkedIn:

LinkedIn does not depend on sharing smart memes or what you've had for breakfast. It is a place to connect with aspiring professionals and potential partners as a home business owner, to develop your customer base, and to accumulate referrals.

Find out more about how LinkedIn runs. If you are not already a member, create a LinkedIn username. Develop a LinkedIn profile that focuses on how other members can be helped by your home company. Your aim is to avoid a ho-hum profile that is dull, and instead create a profile that draws people to you.

Consider building a company profile on LinkedIn for your home business. As you complete the resume portion of your personal LinkedIn profile, you will have the opportunity to set up a business page. In your profile, your company page will be automatically connected to the resume.

You can get started on selling yourself and your home business to other LinkedIn members with these LinkedIn basics in place.

Passive LinkedIn Marketing:
Building relationships and keeping your account updated to convince potential customers, employers, and partners that you are easy to reach and reference is important to set up a good LinkedIn profile. The passive strategy of simply

preserving your profile will lead to the following possibilities:

Exposure to individuals looking for goods or services. The search functions of LinkedIn allow those who are searching for what you give to find your profile and browse your offerings.

Introductions to potential customers. While investigating and messaging potential customers, you can view the references and contacts of your friends and colleagues. Show suggestions on LinkedIn from others. You will showcase testimonials for you and your home company as part of your public profile. These job ethics, product, or service reviews will provide reputation that allows individuals to do business with you.

Proactive LinkedIn Marketing:
You can promote your home business in the following ways to proactively leverage LinkedIn's power:

Post periodic status changes. Write about what you are working on and with whom you are working. Include updates to your target clients and consumers that will be of interest. Rely on how you help people accomplish their objectives.

Taking part in parties. Join groups linked to your home business and your interests on LinkedIn. Participation in discussions will help develop you as an expert in your profession. Don't spam or talk about yourself forever. Rather, answer questions and be a resource that can be trusted by people.

Connect with others in your network and other members of your community. You can communicate with professionals who have common interests by sending customized messages or who can support you in your home business journey.

Try ads on LinkedIn. Paid LinkedIn ads is an opportunity for rapidly bringing your home business in front of potential customers.

Upgrade to a subscription with paid LinkedIn. There are several levels to choose from that will unlock additional opportunities for interaction and other advantages that might be a good match for what you are trying to achieve with your home company. To check before committing, LinkedIn provides a free trial of their paid features.

Adding LinkedIn to Your Plan for Marketing:

Adding LinkedIn to your marketing plan will help you grow your network, find clients/customers, and develop your home business with a professional reputation. Consider attaching your website or blog with a LinkedIn badge, so visitors can quickly find your profile and interact with you.

Email Marketing:

Email marketing includes delivering informative or enjoyable material and promotional messages to individuals who voluntarily subscribe to you to receive your messages. The primary objective is to deepen the relationship with the client or prospect by sending them customized marketing messages. You can also use email marketing to cultivate leads with content that pushes them along the path of the customer by moving the concept forward.

You must remain compliant with GDPR, the CAN-SPAM Act, and other email regulations, depending on your venue. They come down at their heart to responsible commercial email sending just send messages from you to people who are expecting (i.e., they have opted in), make it easy for them to opt out, and when you make contact, be clear about who you are.

The first thing you will need to do with that in mind is strategize how you're going to create your email list, the contact database to which you can send emails. The most popular mechanism is on your website via lead capture forms. Then, to send, track, and monitor the effectiveness of your emails, you will need email marketing software and a CRM.

Word of Mouth Marketing:

Word of mouth marketing is a brand's feedback from clients/customers, which is today's most trusted form of marketing. You need to remain laser-focused on creating the best product or service possible and delivering top-notch customer service to generate as much word-of-mouth marketing as possible. In other words, you need to represent the interests of your clients/customer population prior to your own. Only then will your clients/customers transform into a loyal, passionate tribe who will refer their friends and family to your brand.

Events Marketing:

For the promotion of a brand, product, or service, event marketing is preparing, arranging, and conducting an event. In-person or online activities can take place, and businesses can either host an event, attend as an exhibitor, or participate as a sponsor. Many companies exploit their specific business expertise to include existing helpful information sessions in return for the cost of entry and the positioning of the brand that results after being seen as an expert on the subject by participants. Alternatively, there might be a pitch at the end of the event to prompt interested attendants to make a purchase, or in accordance with that technique.

Influencer Marketing:
Now a days, many individuals are rising to fame by developing a niche of their own, posting exciting content and garnering following of their own. Brands are using this to benefit them. They find a celebrity or an influencer who most resonates with them and uses them to advertise their product. If you are a clothing brand, find a fashion enthusiast, if you are in the gaming department, find a gamer! After narrowing down your potential influencers who could market your product, make an excel sheet. Write down their names and cost of doing a paid advertisement. Write down their number of followers too to determine their reach and now find the best match for your brand. Remember our aim here is to get the most impressions by spending least. Why influencer marketing is so beneficial is that when people here their favorite blogger/

Youtubers recommend a product, they already feel a sense of familiarity and thus are more inclined to buy your product.

Don't forget to stay up to date with new budding influencers and applications. Recently, twitch and TikTok have been major source of advertisements for brands due to their more creative and engaging content.

Chapter 6: The Do's and Don'ts of Brand Building

You can still boost your reputation and step up the ladder, no matter what sort of work or profession you have chosen. Building your personal brand and positioning yourself as an expert in your field is one of the best ways to increase your value to the business and become an asset that they would want to hold. Here are eight ways to make more money and create your personal brand.

1. Start a Blog for the Industry.

Starting a blog is the perfect way to develop your personal brand. They think of musings and everyday updates while other people think of blogs. That is not the case with the best bloggers. You need to find a focus that you understand and become an expert in the field to create a genuinely entertaining blog so that people want to know what you have to say. You are the expert already, by developing a blog inside your field.

And you're not going to have to do it alone. Find places where you don't have total working knowledge and find guest posts that can help your audience understand all aspects. You can also study these areas and blog about the method yourself. By providing insight into every aspect of your business, you create a blog that is a must-stop for industry professionals and position yourself as a space leader. Plus, by digging in and exploring certain areas you are not familiar with, you get the added bonus of studying and developing your skills outside of a classroom.

And the best component? Bloggers who are industry-leading can make a nice side income or even make blogging a full-time work. Targeted blogs have the best conversion rates and can give the industry the highest advertisement rates. And even though you don't post commercials, you become a better worker who can do more. You have a much clearer path to going up the ladder to a better paid job with additional responsibilities when you understand the market and what is happening outside your role.

2. Create Your Accounts on Social Media.
Although the easiest way to develop your brand can be through a blog, your social media profiles are also the fastest. Place yourself on Facebook, LinkedIn, & Twitter as an expert in your room. To keep up with all the news inside your business, follow, friend, and communicate with industry experts and use social media. Twitter is a perfect platform for curating the most influential players.

LinkedIn makes sure you can communicate with those players and network with them. And Facebook gives you a chance to communicate and engage in constructive conversation on a more intimate level with co-workers, managers, etc. Also, when you create accounts on all social media platforms, it will become hard for you to respond to customer queries on all of them, hence use the preinserted messages to respond to customers. This is chat bot which lets customers know if you are away and when they will likely get an answer. This helps to keep the response rate soaring and your page appears more active.

Create your accounts wisely and ensure you regularly share the content of your blog. You will easily put yourself as an expert in the industry who is worth following.

3. Network. Outside of Work, Join Communities. Companies and workers are all too frequently stifled by what they know. They do the same stuff they have always done and expect the same outcomes they have always had. And while this can work, you must get beyond the bubble of information that exists in your industry and tap into the abundance of knowledge available beyond those four walls if you want to become a true thought leader.

Attend networking activities, find meet-up parties, and coffee with individuals in other businesses that perform your job. Shop for Chat. Find out what they do, what works, and what doesn't work for them. Find individuals who work in entirely different fields who have similar challenges and see how they handle them. For instance, if you're the marketing director at a pet store, find someone at an email marketing company who does marketing and find out how they get customers. You can discover something that refers to your business.

4. Take Extra Lessons or Lectures.

For some, learning through experience will work, but others need a direction. It can be extremely beneficial to take extra courses at the local college or training courses from an organization in your market. Your new employer will also pay for these benefits, making your choice a no-brainer! Yes, knowing more will assist them, but it benefits you the most. You can have a greater chance of going up quickly by being a more well-rounded employee who takes initiative. And they would be much more likely to make sure you stick around when an employer invests in your education, which may lead to raises and promotions.

5. Attend Meetings & Trade Shows.

And lastly, don't forget about trade shows and conferences. This is also the one time a year where everybody in your industry is important in one place. And don't just attend the shows and the workshops. After the sessions are done, plan meetings, meals, coffee, and beverages. Outside the walls of the trade-show floor, visit the suppliers and get down to what goods really sell. As much as you can, drink up! At conferences, I have received job opportunities and made lifelong connections that support me to this day.

6. Flexibility:

Flexibility is another do. There should always be room for adjustment in your endeavors. Nothing should be set in stone. Not your tag line and not your logo. If you want to establish a long standing, you must keep changing yourself with the changing of times. New people in new eras would want to see new things and newer preferences and thus your brand must change itself accordingly. Modernize your identity, your ambassadors, your ad campaigns to hook the audience. During corona, a lot of brand started to use the masks and social distancing as props to their ad campaigns this made their content more relatable. Similarly, with *Bridgerton*, the new Netflix period drama on the rise to fame, *SNL* invited Rege-Jean Page to host. The purpose is again, to keep the audience beguiled.

7. Language:

Your league on all platforms be it for advertising or social media or communication must remain consistent, online, and offline. Don't give any mixed signals. You should be delivering the same messages across platforms. But his language should also stay true to your brand. If you are a high-end brand, it is better to stick to professional language. If you are more laidback, adopt a more conversation style. Share your story like we talked about before. This allows for connection to form and emotions to be provoked, share experiences. Share customer stories. Craft and curate your tone.

8. Don't Copy:

Never copy your competition. If you are two brands of the same lamp, then why would the customer bother buying from you. Keep researching. Keep innovating. Keep looking for ways to diversify yourself. Enter new realms of artistically creativity to set yourself apart. You should be one of a kind. A copy never succeeds. Besides copying is plagiarism and you could be legally tested too if it's something that the brand has trademarked.

9. Monitor Your Brand:

Monitoring your brand in terms of profit and loss is important but measuring its social growth, brand recall, identity and more so also important. So, make use of any list ice and tracking bots. These will save data of users that visit your webpage, and you will have an idea of what kind of audiences and customers interact with your business. You will know their age, location, education, interests, gender, relationship status and so much more. This will help you in further curating your ad to ensure that they hit the right spot. Moreover, this will also let you know about which of your marketing strategy worked best for you. It may be a video, a photo, a story which people interacted more with as compared to other posts. Hence, you just need to replicate that success with other posts to keep engagement high. Another thing monitoring helps you with is never losing track of trends and your competition.

You stay a step ahead. There are different ways in which these analytics save data. It may be number of impressions, clicks, searches, likes, saves, message texts, and more. This gives you a unique opportunity to try the A/B split test too. This is usually carried out when people want to try a new marketing ploy. For example, you have a picture with a strong story in the caption but mediocre visuals, and then a post with a mediocre caption but strong visuals. You post both the things at the same time, and the analytics can help you decide which worked better, hence further improving your marketing strategies. You can do this with products too to see which product is better received. There are many performance metrics which can help you decide these. The common ones include Google analytics and Facebook pixel. Both of these store user data. In fact, many use these analytics on their site too. Using these analytics on your site has other advantages. Not only does it help store user data, but it also tells you which user interacted with which product. How much time did they spend on the site, and what they had in their cart? Thai information is crucial since you can use to retarget and target the customer. You can use email marketing to show them a discount on that specific product to encourage to make a purchase.

Other things which can help you are surgery's, comments, reviews, feedbacks and more. Reddit is a platform where tons of social media discussions take place. You can visit there to see what kind of feedback your brand is getting.

10. Paid Advertisements:
All social media platforms allow you to do paid advertisements. All you have to do is lay a small sum of money. However, you have got to be smart about this because you don't want to spend too much. Choose posts carefully that you want to be published for the world to see. Allocate a separate budget for these activities. And the most important part of it all is to finely filter your audience. Write in every little detail of your predicted, targeted customers so you get the bang for your buck. Your ad is only seen by potential customers and hence, no input is wasted. There are great features on Facebook and Instagram which let you finely tune your target audience. Write their city, age, gender, likes, activates and more. Lastly, even after someone sees your ad, they might briefly see your ad, interact with your site a little and not purchase anything. First time

visitors rarely purchase which is why you need to target and retarget them again. This will be easy because you already will have their data stored. A way to do this is by Ad Funneling. Ad funneling allows you to make scheduled posts. These will be showed to the chosen people at selected times of the day with intervals in between. It's a great strategy which always results in conversions. All the platforms have a bunch of formats of advertising be it carousel, video, banner. Find the one which makes your brand tick!

Chapter 7: Brand Integrity

To have a successful brand, brand integrity is essential, but sometimes its limits can be unclear. It's important to find out and introduce ways you can keep your brand known and trusted by people. Then read on to learn three examples of honesty and why it matters if you are looking for advice to ensure that your company retains its integrity.

Brands Consistency:
Efficient branding builds visibility for your company through continuity. Brand consistency ensures that in all contexts, the brand is portrayed in the same way. For example, when designing your graphics for social media, your brand should retain the same branding across all online channels, such as using the same hex colors. In addition, use the voice of your brand and maintain a clear schedule for social media and blog posts to be consistent with contact. Finally, provide consistent goods, including visual presentation, production, and product experience, for customers.

Reputation:
A necessary part of a successful company is establishing and sustaining a positive image. By

consistently behaving with honesty in all your business activities, the best way to build and preserve the credibility of your company is. Bad customer service and inconsistency with product experience are factors that negatively impact the reputation of a company. A bad reputation emerges as word-of-mouth criticism, reports to a better company office, or negative online reviews. Negative reviews can be terribly harmful to the retention and acquisition of clients/customers, so clean them up as quickly and as thoroughly as you can by reacting in a solution-oriented way to negative reviews.

Honesty:
It is authenticity that is part of having brand credibility. Being truthful means pursuing your promises, being open about your market practices, and portraying your goods accurately. Since it builds trust, brand authenticity matters. If your clients/customer population perceive a difference in what you portray and your acts, then you are going to lose their trust. If you behave without honesty and lie by omission, such as having unethical environmental policies, when the unethical practice is made public, the clients will lose faith in you. If your conduct causes your

company's reputation to be undermined, then own up to your error, apologize, and propose a solution.

Choices may often be arbitrary in business. When making your business choices, having things like those above in mind will help make those decisions easier. It's always better to ask a colleague, mentor, or someone you trust who has more experience than you do if you find yourself uncertain if your organization is going to behave without honesty. Brand credibility is a serious thing, and if your company is to be profitable, it's important to keep it up.

How Do You Keep Your Brand Value and Positive Outlook?
For the long-term success of any business, including yours, improving brand equity is crucial.

Create Your Brand with Emotional Ties:
Based in part on their emotional response to products, customers make buying decisions. They want to connect and make them feel better about themselves with a business that is aligned with their beliefs and goals. Why is Apple dominating? Effective businesses are responding to customers' emotional stimuli. Microsoft concentrated on selling characteristics in the old Macintosh vs PC

ads, and then Apple came in and appealed to the urge of the user to be cool and innovative. That is why Apple is so popular.

Internally Reinforcing Your Brand Marketing Plan:

There is a lot of talk these days about the significance of creating a solid, optimistic company culture and guiding employees, particularly online, to act as advocates or ambassadors. But many businesses do not spend the time and training required to make workers feel linked and understand the values of the brand. Online retailer Zappos is an exception, however. For customers and workers, every aspect of the experience is about creating satisfaction. The employees understand that, and on their website, it comes through. Employees in short videos model the shoes, and it's obvious they love the brand.

Transparency and continuous collaboration are one key to building internal brand advocacy. For internal communication, you can choose to use software like Trello. It's better than all those emails floating around one-to-one.

A business that creates a strong emotional bond with its employees also has the ability to showcase its profile with the aid of its employees on different social media channels. Some organizations allow their staff to blog about them, tweet about them, or share information on their Facebook pages. They are also going to protect the business from naysayers.

Maintain Focus and Continuity for the Brand:
They have to know what it means for clients to understand your brand. It is recommended that you show restraint and avoid the temptation to go after possibilities that dilute your name. Business owners often develop an online content plan on their website to boost sales, and then they read a search engine optimization (SEO) article and decide to divert half of their budget to it.

Trends in sales and marketing will still change with the times. Constructing the power of the brand of your business, however, is a solid investment that will pay dividends for years to come.

What Does It Mean When Brand Integrity Is Compromised?
Here's the thing: within your organization, the brand does not exist in a silo. It is uncontrollable and fluid. When you let your brand out of the bag, your customers and everyone else who is exposed to it now belong to them.

It is harder and more critical than ever to maintain the reputation of your brand in a world of short attention spans, remote jobs, high service demands, and digital channels built to proliferate the message of average Joe and Joanne.

It can be hard to separate the buzzwords from the terms worth paying attention to, with so much content, data, and opinions saturating all we consume. The first instance which comes to mind? Integrity of Brand.

Integrity is at significant risk of death by overuse, like words such as "authenticity" and "innovation." Which is a shame, really, that the reputation of the brand is so necessary to preserve for any brand's continued success. You may not know what brand integrity entails, but if you saw it, you would surely accept it (or notice if it was missing). So, you certainly want to ensure that people recognize that honesty rather than a lack of it when it comes to your own brand.

Why Brand Integrity Matters?
In essence, brand integrity means keeping the brand on the spot.

Think of the following components of any brand:

- Brand marks

- Color Palette

- Packaging

- Social Media Presence

- Website

- Key Messages

- Brand Voice

- Brand Reputation and Behavior

- Collateral Branded

- Ads and Marketing Strategies

They lead to the brand image in a positive way when all of these are held in check. And your reputation is therefore improved in exchange. That means maintaining clear design features, aligning the voice of your brand, and coherent action of your brand in every avenue facing the audience. A few more advantages of brand honesty include:

- Asserting your position as a trusted brand

- Strengthening your relationship with your audience, clients, and customers

- Attracting new customers or clients

- Growing the authenticity of your brand

- Building upon your exclusive points of sale

So, what are the possible negatives of the lack of credibility of the brand? Basically, they are the opposite of those incredible advantages. If any of those fundamental things are contradictory, the credibility of your brand is undermined, making the picture and reputation of your brand suffer.

Conclusion:

Branding is a standardized approach used to create recognition and expand consumer loyalty. A mandate from the top and willingness to invest in the future are needed. Branding is about seizing every chance to demonstrate why individuals should prefer one brand over another. The reasons why businesses leverage branding are a willingness to lead, outpace the market, and give workers the best tools to reach consumers.

Branding is an unquestionably effective operation, according to experts, leading an industry as an enterprise, outpacing rivalry, motivating employees. This power becomes apparent when you understand what a brand is, how it is produced, and the measurable returns that come from investing in branding.

The list of benefits never ends. Smoother sales, improved customer satisfaction, the multifaceted advantages of brand equity and what not. At the end of the day, however, the way the world perceives your business is your brand. Therefore, start today. I hope you found something valuable from this book. I wish you the best of luck on this journey. Remember that failures are only opportunities to grow, so keep striving!

P.S. If you would like to take my branding course, titled "Brand Morphing" please visit www.Cloeluv.com

Made in the USA
Coppell, TX
29 July 2022

80627611R00069